D1319854

THE TEN COMMANDMENTS FOR THE LOCAL GOVERNMENT EMPLOYEE

AND OTHER RULES FOR SUCCESS IN ANY CITY OR COUNTY ORGANIZATION

Roman R. Abeyta

authorHOUSE®

AuthorHouse™
1663 Liberty Drive
Bloomington, IN 47403
www.authorhouse.com
Phone: 1-800-839-8640

First published by AuthorHouse   7/15/2009

ISBN: 978-1-4389-6207-8 (sc)

Library of Congress Control Number: 2009906707

Printed in the United States of America
Bloomington, Indiana

This book is printed on acid-free paper.

Acknowledgments

A special thank you to Benjie Montano and Gilbert Chavez for giving an 18 year old a break. Thank you to Santa Fe County Commissioners Jack Sullivan, Paul Campos, Virginia Vigil, Harry Montoya, and Mike Anaya for having the confidence to appoint me Santa Fe County Manager in October 2006.

I would like to thank the following people, without whose support throughout the years my success in local government would not have been possible: Linda Grill, Richard Anaya, Joe Grine, Paul Duran, Marcos Trujillo, Senator Nancy Rodriguez, Asenath Kepler, Gerald Gonzales, Vincent "Corky" Ojinaga, Diana Lucero, Gil Tercero, Estevan Lopez, Oralynn Guerrerortiz, Santa Fe Mayor David Coss, Lynn Canning, Oliver Garcia,

Sevastian Gurule, Laura Banish, Julie Berman, Kathy Holian, Liz Stefanics, and the late Samuel Montoya.

A special thank you to former County Commissioner, and President of the National Association of Counties (NACO) Javier M. Gonzales for the kind words in the Foreword.

To my family, I love each and every one of you. Roberta and Joe Cole, Adi and Estevan Gonzales, Adi Shakti, Amado and Kelly Abeyta, Juan "Buddy" Abeyta, my mom Jennie Salazar, my dad John "Chris" Abeyta.

Thank you to my cousins Joe Abeyta and John Michael Salazar for the many words of encouragement and advice over the years.

Thank you to my cousin Jonathon and his wife Marissa Salazar for taking a first look at the manuscript and suggesting changes.

To my wife Geraldine, you are my support and you always pick me up when I am down. You encourage me to take chances. You are strong and beautiful. To my boys Roman, Jacob, Dillon, Joshua and Jimmy, you guys are my inspiration.

And last but not least, thank you to my grandpa Roman Salazar. When he found out I was having my first child he insisted that I get a job in government.

(Ps 16:7, John 3:16, Phil 4:13, Ps 23, 1Cor. 13)

FOREWORD

Inevitably, every organization delivers the diamond out of coal. In the case of Santa Fe County, Roman Abeyta is the shiny diamond, with county government being the coal mine. I had the privilege of serving as a Santa Fe County commissioner from 1995–2002. During those years, we transformed county government from a sleepy bureaucracy to a thriving government focused on delivering services in a customer-friendly efficient manner. Little did I realize at the time that there was a young man who had quietly been working his way up the governance structure and one day would end up leading one of the state's largest and fastest-growing counties. During my term as county commissioner, I was also elected to lead the National Association of Counties. That opportunity allowed me the chance to visit with some of the most successful and dynamic government executives across the country. Each had their own style of governance that led to their success. However, rarely have I met an individual with the passion and love of public service that Roman has demonstrated to the people of Santa Fe County. He in all respects can relate to every level of government because of his vast experience in public service. Whether it is as an animal control officer or county manager, he's been there. It is because of his experience, passion, and love of civil service that he is unconditionally one of the finest county executives in the country. Roman understands that the truest kind of leadership demands service and selflessness. He has a servant's heart and exemplifies sacrifice. He has the character to motivate people to follow. After fifteen years in government, I thought I knew almost everything a true leader possessed until I read *The Ten Commandments for the Local Government Employee*. Roman brings a pragmatic approach to successful government leadership. Following his commandments will assure that every government leader will have the right work/life balance, maintain positive influence over their organization, and manage the difficult political environment. I assure you that even the most experienced leader will find value in reading this book as will that first-year employee. This book is for everyone. I hope you enjoy it and learn from it as much as I have.

Javier M. Gonzales

To Geraldine.
Thank you for believing in me.
I love you.

Contents

Introduction

I have worked in local government for eighteen years. I began my career when I was eighteen years old in Santa Fe County, New Mexico, as an animal control officer. Over fifteen years, I worked my way up to the highest position in the county, county manager. Today, as manager, I have come to realize that the basic things in local government—or shall I say the things that *should* be basic: treating the public good, working hard, and being always willing to go above and beyond the call of duty—apply whether you are a animal control officer at the bottom of the local government organizational chart or a county or city manager.

As I moved up through the ranks, I noticed that working for local government became more and more difficult. For example, having to supervise employees was difficult, and being exposed more to the political side of local government at times seemed too much to handle. I reached a point in my career where I began to question why I was doing this and whether I could continue. At first, I justified continuing for the retirement. At Santa Fe County, we have a twenty-five-year retirement plan, and when I started questioning myself I was more than halfway there. It wasn't long, though, before I started asking myself the question again. A cozy retirement wasn't enough to counter the effects of the sleepless nights before I had to discipline an employee or when I observed (and in some cases participated in) political paybacks. Both were having an effect on my peace of mind. I decided that retirement wasn't worth it. As I contemplated leaving local government, I was asked to become the deputy county manager. In this position, I would have new challenges, such as being in charge of the day-to-day operations for the entire county, not just one department.

One of my new duties as deputy county manager was to introduce new hires to the county and tell them what kind of organization they had just joined. The best way I could explain the type of organization they were joining was to share my story with them—how I worked my way up from animal control to deputy county manager. This was the kind of organization Santa Fe County was. This is the kind of organization most local governments are. Local governments throughout the country are organizations where today's accountant, custodian, or public safety official is tomorrow's city or county manager. New employees really responded to such potential for advancement, so much so that we started using it at Santa Fe County as a recruitment tool. Our slogan was, "At Santa Fe County, today's animal control officer is tomorrow's county manager." Employees started seeking me out to ask me how they could advance and if there was a secret to my success. Then it dawned on me: Maybe this is why I'm not finished in local government yet. Working at Santa Fe County had always been about helping the public, but now maybe it could also be about helping the employees.

Today, my inspiration—my passion—is to help other local government employees working in cities and counties across the country be successful. City and county employees provide a service to the public that the public cannot get anyplace else. We are underpaid and underappreciated, and we have to deal with circumstances that are unique to us. I wrote this book to reach out to as many city and county employees as possible, so that they have someplace to turn, a book to read, that tells them they are not alone and that somebody else has been there and understands what they are dealing with. My message is not to give up; it is possible to have a successful, rewarding career in local government.

I compiled this book of advice based on my own personal experiences in local government. I enjoy a successful life both personally and professionally thanks to a solid foundation I built years ago following the many rules and lessons contained in the Bible, specifically the Ten Commandments from the Old Testament. With that in mind, I have written what I call "The Ten Commandments for the Local Government Employee," which I believe form a solid foundation for a very successful career in local government. Like anything else in this life, once you have built a solid foundation in city or county government, the sky is the limit. That is why I also include advice in this book for middle and senior managers. I hope you enjoy this quick read, share it with other local government employees, and continue to refer and practice its principles throughout your career.

PART I: THE TEN COMMANDMENTS FOR THE LOCAL GOVERNMENT EMPLOYEE

Thou shall love thy job with all thy heart, soul, and mind.

Treat the public as you would like to be treated. Thou shall always treat the public with courtesy and respect.

Thou shall work diligently five days a week, but days off are for you and your family.

Thou shall honor the governing body and elected officials.

Thou shall treat thy fellow employees how you want to be treated.

Thou shall not covet thy boss's position.

1

Thou shall seek career development through hard work and educational training.

Thou shall not misuse thy position in local government.

Thou shall not place thy personal ambitions above the wellbeing of the organization.

Thou shall not participate in political activities.

COMMANDMENT I: "THOU SHALL LOVE THY JOB WITH ALL THY HEART, SOUL, AND MIND."

If you don't love your job in local government, you need to start looking for someplace else to work. We spend too much of our lives working not to love what we are doing. So I guess you can say that this commandment applies anywhere you choose to work.

I started working for Santa Fe County when I was eighteen years old. I didn't start to work for Santa Fe County out of choice but rather out of necessity. This was the summer after I graduated from high school and my first son was born. I married his mother and needed a job with benefits. My mother happened to work in the Human Resources Department at Santa Fe County, and there happened to be an opening for an animal control officer. I applied, got the job, and hated it. I only had to work there for five months, but that five months seemed like an eternity. When you don't like your job, time seems to drag along.

I had no intentions of being an animal control officer. I was doing what I had to do, not what I wanted to. I woke up every work morning dreading going to work. I was miserable, working only because I was married and had a child I needed to take care of. One day while answering a dog-running-at-large call, I was bit on the hand. That was it for me. I started applying for any position that opened up in the county.

Five months later, after a failed attempt to get a different position in the County Tax Assessor's Office, I got hired for a position in the Land Use and Planning Department. It was an entry-level position reviewing building permit applications for zoning compliance. I didn't know much about land use and zoning, but I took it anyway. At that point, I thought that anything would be better than animal control. It's not as if I had anything against animal control; it just wasn't for me.

Land use was a completely different story. From the day I started to the day I left the department, twelve years later, I loved my job. Land use and community planning is a field where you are constantly learning and being challenged. During the 1990s, development in Santa Fe County exploded, so the department was always expanding and there was plenty of opportunity for advancement. I didn't know what I was getting into by joining this department, but I found it very exciting and challenging. It didn't take much for me to put everything I had into it. I started out in the Land Use and Planning Department as a building plan reviewer. When I left, I was the planning and land use director. Today, reflecting on my years in land use and my months in animal control, it seems as if the five months I spent in animal control lasted longer than the twelve years I spent in land use. When you love your job, time flies by.

In government, the benefits—such as health insurance, vacation, and retirement—are among the best in the country, especially the retirement plans. Today, many people are leaving the private sector for government jobs, because they are more stable and the retirement plans are sound. However, it doesn't take these individuals very long to realize that the challenges in local government are very difficult. The public, employees, and politics are probably the hardest things to get used to. Today, I share this first commandment and my own personal experience with my bosses and staff in an attempt to help. In many local governments it takes twenty to twenty-five years for somebody to retire, and that's a long time to spend there if you're not working someplace you love.

Commandment II: "Treat the public as you would like to be treated. Thou shall always treat the public with courtesy and respect."

This is the most widely known and preached commandment in city and county governments throughout the country, and yet it is also the least obeyed. I once attended a customer service training session where the instructor explained why customer service is so bad in government: government is the only place the public can go to get what they need. So in essence government has a monopoly on the services it provides. He was absolutely right. There's only one place you can go to get your business license or call when you need that pot hole in the street repaired. In local government, we are not competing with the guys across the street for business, so it's not like we're going to be shut down and lose our jobs because people are going somewhere else for the services we provide. Some advice for treating the public as you would like to be treated includes: (a) always return phone calls and e-mail requests the day you receive them, and (b) get back to the public when you say you are going to.

At the top of any city or county's organizational chart is the public. Right below the public are the elected officials, then the manager/administrator, then the staff. The higher up you go in government, the more you understand the importance of treating the public with courtesy and respect, but ironically it's the staff down at the lowest level of the organizational chart that deal with the public most. There lies the reason why obeying this commandment will result in a successful career in local government. When the elected officials and staff at the top of the organizational chart are out in public, they are going to hear about the experience a constituent had at the city or county they represent. There will usually be a name of an employee attached to it. If it's your name, you want to make sure it was a positive experience.

When I first started working for the county at eighteen, my grandfather made it very clear to me that government was there to serve the public, not the other way around. I have been very successful in local government, because many years ago I developed a reputation at Santa Fe

County as "go-to guy" when you needed help. I always went the extra mile for the public. After a while, county commissioners started sending people to me for help. It wasn't that I was going to find a way to get their constituents what they wanted, but it was that even if I couldn't give the constituent what they wanted, the commissioners were confident that I would be able to communicate clearly why, and what the other options were. After meeting with me, a member of the public might still have left upset, but he was leaving upset with the rules that didn't allow him to get what he wanted, not the county.

Today, as county manager, I emphasize to all my employees that in local government customer service skills are just as important as any other skill somebody can possess. The engineer's certificate, education, and experience doesn't mean much if the person who has it can't communicate with the public and doesn't treat the public right. There will always be room on my staff for the employee whose only skill is providing good customer service, because I know that getting the right technical training is much easier than teaching someone how be good to the public.

It doesn't matter what department you work for in local government; you still have to treat the public with courtesy and respect. Even if you work as a correctional officer in the county jail, you are still interacting with the taxpayer and providing a service. I have received numerous calls over the years from family members of inmates stating how rudely they were treated just because their son or daughter was in jail. I've even heard from inmates themselves about how they were treated. Not all people in jail are there because they are bad, they may have done something bad, but their families don't deserve to be punished for it.

It's always helped me to put myself in the public's shoes. When I need to visit a state agency for something, such as a copy of my son's birth certificate for baseball registration, I ask myself, how would I want to be treated? Regardless of where we work in local government, we need to remember that we are employed by the taxpayer to provide a service for them. Also, whether we like it or not, we are a reflection of the government and elected officials we work for. Sometimes we are a taxpayer's only experience with the city or county we work for, and how we treat them will determine what they think about our organization. If you want to be successful in local government, the impression you leave with people about the city or county you work for needs be a positive one.

COMMANDMENT III: "THOU SHALL WORK DILIGENTLY FIVE DAYS A WEEK, BUT DAYS OFF ARE FOR YOU AND YOUR FAMILY."

Eight hours a day, five days a week, is plenty of time to get your work done at a city or county. If you are not getting work done in that amount of time and have to stay late or take home work on the evenings and weekends on a regular basis, something is wrong. You are probably either spending too much time hanging out with co-workers during the day or you are not organized. I'm married and have five sons, so I have never been able to take work home, and yet over the years I have continued to rise to the top. Yes, many times I've been tempted to take work home or come in on the weekend because I've fallen behind on e-mails or returning phone calls, but I learned that all it takes to catch up is to come in twenty minutes before work starts, or to work through the lunch hour.

The higher you advance at the city or county, the more important this commandment becomes. As you advance at the city or county, the more difficult and stressful the job becomes. Once you become a supervisor, don't be afraid to delegate work. I once read somewhere that whenever you have multiple tasks at the same time, the first thing you need to do is prioritize the tasks and then review each one and ask yourself if somebody else can do it. If the answer to that question is yes and you have the authority to delegate it to somebody else, you should. As county manager, when I assign a specific task or project to a department, I make it a point to remind that director not to be afraid to delegate. When I ask for something, I expect it to be taken care of in a timely manner, and it's more important to me that it get done rather than the director doing it him or herself. The ability to delegate is one I look for in a department director. It shows that the director has a staff that listens to her and will get the job done for her.

It's also important to remember that the higher you advance in your career, the less technical and hands-on the work will be that you are expected to produce. There are positions at the top of every organization where you will be paid more for your ability to think, direct, lead, and make tough decisions than to actually produce reports or fix the air conditioning unit yourself. At the end of the day, regardless of where you are in the organizational structure at the city or county, no one position is more important than the other.

Even if you aren't married and don't have kids, there is more to life than work. Over the years, I have learned the importance of having a good work-home life balance. In life, you have to allow time for work, time for exercise, time for play, and time for rest. An honest eight hours a day, five days a week, is plenty of time for work. Enjoy your days off and don't spend your time off thinking about work. When you start to think about work, change your mind and think about something else. It really is that simple. Whether you are county administrator or an animal control officer, at the end of the day it is just a job.

Commandment IV: "Thou shall honor the governing body and elected officials."

The county commissioners, city councilors, and other elected officials have worked hard to get elected and must continue to work hard to be re-elected. Even if you don't agree with their views on the issues, they ran for office to make a difference in the community you live in and are willing to devote their time and energy to this, and that should be honored and respected.

In most local governments a majority vote is required for a decision to be made. A common mistake that some city and county employees will make is to pay attention only to the commissioners or councilors who they perceive make up that majority. Don't ever get caught up in trying to figure out who's in the majority and who's not. In local government, the majority changes from time to time and also can change from issue to issue. A clear majority gets even harder to figure out when you have a governing body with lots of officials. Just do your job; treat each member of the governing body with the same level of respect and you'll be successful no matter who's in the majority.

Early in my career I noticed that there was a clear majority on the five member County Commission at that time. This majority was made up of four commissioners, and the higher-ups always paid attention only to them and not to the one who was in the minority. The four members of the board ignored him, the directors ignored him, and even the line staff would ignore him. Eventually another election rolled around, as they tend to every two years in most local governments, and two of these four commissioners were unseated. Suddenly this one commissioner found himself split between the two new commissioners and the two commissioners remaining from the old majority. He became the swing vote, a position even more powerful than a member of the majority. Guess what happened? He sided with the two new incoming commissioners and the three of them fired the county manager and all the department directors. The line staff that ignored him would have been gone too if they weren't in classified positions. Although the line staff was left alone, those who went out of their way to ignore this commissioner's requests now found themselves having to go out of their way to meet his requests. That's not a position you ever wanted to find yourself in. Honor each member of the governing body and all elected officials with respect and you won't ever have to worry about who's going to be in office or out of office.

COMMANDMENT V: "THOU SHALL TREAT THY FELLOW EMPLOYEES HOW YOU WANT TO BE TREATED."

Never gossip about a fellow employee. Never be rude to a fellow employee. Always be willing to provide assistance to a fellow employee. Always be willing to show your co-worker how to do your job. We spend too much time at work not to get along with the people we work with. Remember, local government usually promotes from within first, so chances are sooner or later your fellow employee is going to be your boss—or even worse, you're going to be his.

Also, what goes around comes around. I have worked with many individuals who were just plain mean to the public and everyone who worked around them. Sometimes these people were in positions of authority and were able to treat their co-workers and subordinates really poorly. I can recall one individual in particular who was rude to everyone she worked with and had the attitude that she was smarter and more important than them. This individual had also developed a reputation for treating the public badly. When there was a change in administration, she knew she would have a difficult time working for the new administration, because she was so entrenched with the outgoing administration. She decided to quit and start up a consulting business because of her experience with the county. Her ex-coworkers saw this as their opportunity to pay her back now that the tables were turned and she needed their help. Needless to say, her business didn't do to well and it wasn't long before she closed shop and ended up working back in government.

I've seen the opposite happen also. Individuals who treat the public and their co-workers well go on to have successful careers as consultants, because they have such good access to information and people at the city or county. Some have even gone on to have successful careers in politics. At Santa Fe County, a number of ex-county employees have gone on to hold both local and statewide elected offices. Every one of them had a reputation for treating the people they worked with and supervised with courtesy and respect.

Commandment VI: "Thou shall not covet thy boss's position."

Throughout your career, your boss's boss will ask you how she's doing. The response should always go something like this: "She's doing great, and she's a good boss!" Even if you don't think your boss is doing a good job and you can do better, there are a million reasons why you are being asked this, but it is never so that they can make you the boss.

At times, you will be asked to cover a meeting for your boss. Be sure to let him or her know about the meeting immediately after you get out. Bosses hate to be surprised. This is even more critical if the meeting is with a member of the governing body or if there is bad news.

In many local governments, the turnover rate for bosses is pretty high. This may be the case at the local government you work for, and if it is, be loyal to your boss while he or she is your boss, and after he or she is gone be loyal to that person's successor. In doing this, you are demonstrating loyalty not only to your boss but to the local government you work for.

Many times you will be asked how *you* are doing. This is not an opportunity to talk about your boss either. You don't need to covet your boss's position. In local government, sooner or later you'll get your chance if you just work hard, treat the public well, and follow the other eight commandments. But as the saying goes, "Be careful what you ask for. Someday you might get it."

COMMANDMENT VII: "THOU SHALL SEEK CAREER DEVELOPMENT THROUGH HARD WORK AND EDUCATIONAL TRAINING."

Develop your skills through hard work and educational training. Do you want to move up to the next level? Find out what the qualifications for the job are and go out and get them. Work hard in your current position, always be willing to go the extra mile without the extra pay, and leave no room for doubt when the position you're after opens up. There is no chicken-or-egg debate here. In local government, hard work comes first; the salary increase and promotion to a higher position follows.

Time and time again I've heard employees say the opposite. Ask most local government employees to take on more work and they will say, "Is there a raise involved?"

When there's no money involved, the employee will add, "I'm too busy to take on extra work anyways." It's amazing how money buys time. Most employees are too busy to take on extra work, but if a salary increase is involved, they'll suddenly be willing to do it. If the boss finds more money, the employee will find more time. A good boss sees through this and will always reward the employee that is willing to take on the extra work or new assignment without asking for more money.

A boss is always looking for individuals in their department that they can take special assignments to and who will do them without any griping. It's these individuals who are looked at first when it comes time for merit increases and promotion. Plus, remember that there is more than one way to reward an employee, and bosses have more at their disposal than just money.

Most if not all local governments provide educational training opportunities for its employees. Take advantage of this. Go to seminars, training sessions, and even get your college degree or advanced degree on the government's tab. The more education and training you have, the more valuable you become to the organization.

Take the time to read books about business success and leadership. Although there isn't much out there specific to local government, most of the principles found in these other books can be applied to what you're doing. Take the time to read books about personal success also. Many of the principles you find in these books can and should be applied to your professional life as well.

COMMANDMENT VIII: "THOU SHALL NOT MISUSE THY POSITION IN LOCAL GOVERNMENT."

Sooner or later, somebody in the public will ask you to do something unethical or illegal. **DO NOT DO IT!** Anybody who asks you to do something like this is just using you.

I have been approached countless times over my career and asked to "look the other way," "help somebody get the contract," or "ease up on the conditions of approval for a permit." Even people who I've known and respected have asked me this. Throughout your career, even people you know and respect will ask this of you. If you really want to help them, the best thing to do is to make sure all the rules are followed and that everything is done right.

Time and again I have explained to staff that if they really want to help somebody out, make sure they follow all the rules. Trying to help somebody out by relaxing certain rules or requirements is actually making it harder for that person in the long run. If they get what they want the right way, they will never have to worry about it again in the future.

This is especially true in the planning and land use field. I spent several years reviewing and processing residential subdivision and zoning applications. Developers were always trying to get around the regulations to save money. I remember working with a developer who was notorious for this, and after a few years I told him that although the applications that I have processed for him at first seemed more difficult, in the long run I saved him a lot of time and money. When he paused to consider this, he agreed. He never had problems with the people he sold lots to in the subdivisions I processed for him, because I made sure they were built right.

Once I was approached to push something for somebody and was told if I helped it would pay off for me personally. This person also insisted that I would be helping the county by doing this. My response to him was to save his money; if what he was providing was indeed good for the county, it would happen all on its own without me having to push it.

COMMANDMENT IX: "THOU SHALL NOT PLACE THY PERSONAL AMBITIONS ABOVE THE WELLBEING OF THE ORGANIZATION."

Once you start to experience success in local government, you may toy with the idea of running for political office. Most cities and counties require an employee running for office to take a leave of absence a few months before the election. I think that if an employee is serious about running for office, she shouldn't just take a leave of absence but should quit her job once she decides to run for office—especially if the seat she is running for is for the governing body or elected office that she currently works for. I have worked with individuals who become candidates for office, and it makes for an uncomfortable working environment. The employees, the bosses, and even the public become uncomfortable. Everybody suddenly has to pay special attention to this individual, because he or she may become their boss or hold a position of power.

I have seen many examples of this over the years at Santa Fe County. At Santa Fe County there are six elected offices: assessor, treasurer, clerk, probate judge, sheriff, and county surveyor. Employees working in one of these offices have often run for the office seat. This always tears the office apart, and it takes a long time after the election to fix. Many times the employees are forced to take a side, and those on the losing side often have to leave what was a good job in local government.

First let's start with the pre-election. There is the signing of nomination petitions, fundraising (such as buying and selling raffle tickets), invitations to rallies, endorsements, and so on. While no candidate will ever admit to asking his or her co-workers or the public for help while on the job, the pressure exists. Then there's the post election. Win or lose, everybody, including the successful candidate, feels awkward. Those who helped the successful candidate feel as if they are owed something, and those that didn't feel as if the new boss will be out to get them. And they may be. Running for office and continuing to work for the same organization is the typical example of putting your personal ambitions above the wellbeing of the organization in local government. If you decide to run, do the right thing and quit your job well in advance of the election. Besides, if you run and you lose, your opponent will become your boss, and chances are it won't be long before you're looking for another job.

Commandment X: "Thou shall not participate in political activities."

The biggest myth in local government is that those who are successful are those who are politically connected. The truth is that those who are successful are those who follow the Ten Commandments for the local government employee. Many employees think because they have attended a political function or two or have worked for the city and county for a long time they understand politics. I can assure you they do not. I have worked for local government for eighteen years, have spent twelve of those years in what may be considered one of the most political departments (planning and land use) at Santa Fe County, I'm going on my fourth year in absolutely the most political position (county manager) in any city or county, and yet not even I consider myself to be an expert in politics.

Do yourself a favor and leave political science to the politicians and the students majoring in it at college. You don't need to know politics, like politics, or participate in political activities to be successful in local government. If you follow the Ten Commandments, the winners and losers of elections will always be irrelevant to your advancement at the city or county.

Over the years working with elected officials, I have learned that their circle of trust is very small. In politics you see the same people at political functions and they usually pledge their support to whomever asks. An elected official knows this, and so he or she will always keep a suspicious eye on the local government employee that participates in political activities.

Some local government employees will choose to participate in political activities anyway and even go as far as to publicly pledge their support for a candidate. This individual is gambling with his or her future. Participating in political activities is like playing roulette with your career. If the marble lands on black and your chips are on red you are going to lose it all. You may be successful in the beginning, get a small raise or promotion for backing the right candidate, but sooner or later a candidate you support will lose an election and you may lose your job.

Furthermore, an elected official won't bet his future on you just because you supported him.

The employee who follows Ten Commandments for the local government employee is more valuable to an elected official than the employee who puts a campaign sign in his yard.

Summary

Commandment I. Thou shall love thy job with all thy heart, soul, and mind.

This first commandment is the most important. You spend too much time of your life working not to love what you are doing. If you don't love your job in local government, you need to start looking for some place else to work. Government work is rewarding but can also be very difficult. If you don't love your job in local government you won't be successful.

Commandment II. Treat the public as you would like to be treated. Thou shall always treat the public with courtesy and respect.

This is the most widely known and preached commandment in local government, yet it is also the least obeyed commandment. Those that obey it are guaranteed to achieve success.

Commandment III. Five days you shall work diligently, but days off are for yourself and your family.

Take your days off and enjoy them. Eight hours a day, five days a week is plenty of time to get the job done in local government if you are really working those 8 hours, five days a week. In local government if you're not getting the job done in eight hours you're probably socializing too much and/or are unorganized.

Commandment IV. Thou shall honor the governing body and elected officials.

Always treat the governing body and elected officials with courtesy and respect. Always treat each individual elected official with the same courtesy and respect. Don't give special attention to the elected officials who are perceived to have the power in the local government.

Commandment V. Thou shall treat thy fellow employees how you want to be treated.

Never gossip about a fellow employee. Never be rude to a fellow employee. Always be willing to provide assistance and training to a fellow employee. Local government usually promotes from within so chances are sooner or later your fellow employee is going to be your boss or even worse you're going to be his.

Commandment VI. Thou shall not covet thy boss's position.

Throughout your career your boss's boss will ask you how she's doing. The response should always go something like this: "She's doing great. She's a good boss!" There are a million reasons they could be asking you this, but it is never so that they can make you the boss. In local government, sooner or later you'll get your chance if you just work hard and treat the public well. But as the saying goes, "Be careful what you ask for. Someday you might get it."

Commandment VII. Thou shall seek career development through hard work and educational training.

There is no chicken-or-egg debate here. In local government hard work comes first, and the salary increases and recognition follow. If you want to move up to the next level, find out what the qualifications for the job are and go out and get them.

Commandment VIII. Thou shall not misuse thy position in local government.

Never accept a kickback or bribe. Ever! Never do something that is illegal or unethical. The most important thing a person can have in this life is a good reputation. In local government, a reputation follows you everywhere you go, so make sure yours is a good one.

Commandment IX. Thou shall not place thy personal ambitions above the wellbeing of the organization.

If you want to run for political office, quit your job before you sign up to run.

Commandment X. Thou shall not participate in political activities.

You don't need to participate in political activities to be successful in local government. Obey the Ten Commandments for the local government employee and you will be successful.

The Ten Commandments are applicable in every level of city and county government.

PART II: SUBMITTING TO AUTHORITY

I teach a leadership series to my employees, and one of the topics is called "Submitting to Authority." This topic is the most controversial and generates the most discussion of all the topics. Some employees will comment that they find the title offensive. When I put the series together, I questioned the title and topic myself because I had a feeling it might be controversial. I decided to include it because I believe that a leader must take risks, and some aspects of leadership and leaders themselves are controversial. Based on my experience in local government, I am certain that one cannot advance into a leadership position in any city or county organization if he or she is not able to submit to authority.

In most cities and counties, there is a chain of command where the employees answer to the supervisors, the supervisors answer to the directors, the directors answer to the city administrator, and the administrator answers to the governing body. Orders and decisions get passed down from the top, from the governing body or county manager, down the organizational chart to the appropriate staff below. The problem with this order of business is that usually the lower level staff has more experience and knowledge in the applicable specialized area than the bosses or elected officials making the decisions or giving the orders. The staff member sees himself as being "smarter" than the boss or bosses when it comes to the issue and may not agree with the decision. A good employee will submit to authority and implement the direction or decision with a smile on his or her face anyway. As a member of the staff, you may not agree with an order you are given or think that the decision that was made is not the right one. You may not be realizing that there is a different view of things from the top. The higher-ups more than likely have taken something into consideration that you cannot see or do not have access to see.

Once when I was having a difficult time with my staff over a decision that I made, I spoke to someone I trust who works for a different agency, and he said to me, "Take it easy. All they are seeing is the plate of food." This guy likes to eat, so I figured he knew what he was talking about, and I asked him to explain that to me further. His explanation went something like this, "As the boss, you get to see all the ingredients that go into preparing the meal. The employee only gets to see the final product you decide to feed them." Remembering that bit of advice, I try to explain to my staff as much as I can about the decision or direction that is being passed down, but unfortunately, I'm not always able to explain things fully. Sometimes a decision has to be made quickly, and they just have to trust me and submit to my authority.

As county manager, I have to submit to the authority of the governing body. Sometimes the governing body doesn't have the time to explain everything to me or may not want to explain everything to me (for example, a political consideration), and I just have to trust that they know what they are doing and implement their decision anyway, without all the facts. Why the decision was made is not as important as how you go about implementing the decision. A good city or county employee is able to take direction and implement decisions without having the "why" always explained to him. More important, a good supervisor will never let her employees know that she does not agree with a directive or decision from above.

Another example of when you may find yourself having to submit to authority in local government is during your annual personnel performance appraisal. The more honest your supervisor or boss is with you about your work performance, the more your ability to submit to authority will be tested. I remember one occasion where an employee came to see me about her annual performance evaluation. She told me that she totally disagreed with her supervisor about the evaluation. I looked it over and told her that I wished more of my supervisors were as honest with their employees as this one was with her. She was stunned. I told her she should be grateful that all of the issues her boss has with her have been identified and now she has a work plan to follow. Plus, if her supervisor is wrong and she is doing well in these areas, then the work plan wouldn't be that difficult to follow and it wouldn't be long before the employee showed dramatic improvement in the areas identified. Next, I suggested that she sign up for my leadership series because there is a section on submitting to authority that she may find beneficial. Her immediate response was that she did not have a problem with submitting to authority. My reply was, "Now that you got your evaluation, we will see if you have a problem submitting to authority or not." She stopped right there and ended the conversation with, "You are right. I'm going to go back to my office now and from this point forward do exactly what my boss says I need to do to improve."

There may be times throughout your career at the city or county when your boss and/or the elected officials will be wrong. When this happens, you need to remember that they are human. They are going to make mistakes. You shouldn't be disappointed to the point that it affects your ability to continue to work hard for them. Without realizing it, we all have a tendency to look at the people in our organizational structure who are in higher positions than ours and put them on a pedestal. We especially do this with those individuals who have been elected to office. They may have the power to set policy, but that doesn't mean they have the expertise. The higher up you are in the organization the more responsible you become to minimizing your boss's mistakes. As the saying goes, "make lemonade with the lemon(s) you were handed." With this being said, there may come a time when you absolutely cannot submit to authority because you are being asked to compromise your morals. If you find yourself in this position, and there are no alternatives, then you may have to leave the city or county. If you decide to leave, do it quietly.

Part III: Middle Management In Local Government

Congratulations, the powers that be finally recognized that you are the best engineer, code enforcement officer, or accountant in your department and have decided to make you a supervisor. What they failed to recognize is that you're going to be doing less and less of the engineering, code enforcement, or accounting work as time goes by. This could be disastrous for both you and the local government you work for. Here is some advice and tips to ensure your success as a middle manager.

As a middle manager, you are important to the City or County organization because

1. You are the bridge of communication between the county or city administrator and line staff.

2. You turn policy into reality.
3. You are responsible for building and maintaining morale.
4. You provide continuity of activity and instant memory.
5. You will someday take on a leadership role for the organization.

The biggest frustrations you will encounter as a middle manager in local government include:

Politics: It's a reality that you will never be able to change. Don't take it personally. I spent many years as a land use planner making recommendations for and against projects based on county codes, and there were many instances when my recommendation seemed to fall on deaf ears. The codes and local ordinances sometimes would not be followed by the governing body, just because of who the applicant knew or had helped on the governing body. I learned a long time ago that it wasn't in my best interest to take this to heart, and I never made the applicant or the commissioners feel as if they had to justify their decision to me. Not all my co-workers shared these same sentiments, and sooner or later they quit out of frustration. As time went by, I became a department director. I wasn't put in this leadership position because I wouldn't recommend denial or follow the codes but because I would treat the applicant and the commissioners well regardless of the outcome of the case I was processing. I didn't take it personally and neither did they. The higher up you go in local government, the more politics and political favors you will be exposed to. Get used to it.

Policy and procedures: You will be expected to provide input and make recommendations in the development of policy and procedures. What you recommend will not always be adopted. The good middle managers are able to implement these policies and procedures that they advised against anyway—and they do it with a smile. Never let the employees that you supervise know you are frustrated or dissatisfied with the administration, your supervisor, or the governing body. If you're not happy with your boss or the governing body, then you need to decide if you want to continue working for that department or if you want to continue working for the city or county.

If you decide to leave the department, don't burn the bridge behind you. A departure should always be quiet, and if anybody asks you, it is because you "want a change." In local government, people's paths may cross several times throughout their careers.

Supervising staff: The hardest thing about being a middle manager is supervising staff. You won't be able to keep everybody happy, so don't bother trying. Always be fair and honest with your staff. They will respect you for it. Reward and discipline staff as appropriate.

You're going to hear about members of your staff talking badly about you sooner or later. Learn to ignore it and treat them good anyway. You talked bad about your boss when you were at the lower levels, so now you're just getting it back.

Don't rely on the city or county to provide adequate supervisory training for you even though this is going to be the most difficult part of your job and will consume most of your time. Seek out management seminars yourself, take classes, and read books on the subject. If nothing else, always remember to be honest with your employee about his or her shortcomings no matter how difficult this is.

Staff morale: As a supervisor for the city or county, you are responsible for your employees' morale. The inability to submit to authority as discussed in Part 2 of the book is one of, if not the single, cause for low morale within a section or department in local government. When one of my supervisors comes to me to complain about morale issues within his staff, I question him as follows:

- What message are you conveying to your staff?
- How are you implementing our policies or direction?
- What kind of attitude do you display to them?
- Are you in any way telling them or showing them that you do not agree with me or the governing body?

If he can honestly answer these questions, he may find that he is causing the bad morale. I remember two employees from the same department challenged me on this subject by stating that the morale in their department was low, but their boss had nothing to do with it. Their boss was the best they said. Knowing their boss better than they did, I know the boss was the problem. (I didn't convey this to them. It would be inappropriate for me as the county manager to put down a higher-ranking member of my staff to his or her subordinates.) After pondering the staff's statements for a day or two, I concluded that staff can easily confuse a good person for a good manager. There's a big difference. In the case of this particular supervisor, she is a kind, loving person, but as a boss shies away from conflict, has trouble making decisions, and has been know to criticize publicly upper management and the Board of County Commissioners.

Other skills and abilities you are going to need to develop as a middle manager include:

A clear understanding of your department's mission, vision, values, and strategic direction: If you don't have clear understandings of these things, don't be afraid to ask. If your department doesn't have a mission or strategic direction, your director will make sure to develop one and will probably ask for your input since you raised the issue.

The ability to communicate and make real the mission and vision, values, and strategic direction to your employees: Don't rely on your boss to communicate goals and direction to your employees. She's probably relying on you to do it.

The ability to manage change and transitions effectively: Department directors, city and county managers, and elected officials come and go. You remain the constant for the lower-level employees, and it is your attitude towards change that the lower-level employees are going to imitate. Always be positive when it comes to change, even if you have doubts about it yourself. Remember, you are loyal to the city or county, and that means you are loyal to whoever your boss is and whoever the elected officials are.

The ability to resolve conflict in an effective manner: As a middle manager, you should try to resolve conflicts without having to get your boss involved. There are conflicts that cannot and should not be solved without your boss's input and involvement, but the more you can handle conflict yourself, the more your boss will appreciate you.

The ability to communicate expectations: When communicating, get straight to the point and don't be afraid to be blunt. Tell your employees exactly what you expect. Allow and create opportunities for your staff to ask questions and provide input. When you assign work, be sure to set deadlines and communicate them clearly. Make sure everyone in your group has a clear understanding of their assignments and deadlines. Follow up and follow through with your employees by recognizing them for their efforts or disciplining them for their lack of effort.

Skills in time management: As a middle manager, you are still going to be expected to perform technical tasks along with the supervising and leading your group or team. Manage your time appropriately. Block out times to complete your own work using your appointment calendar.

The ability to organize priorities: The most important skills for a supervisor are organizational skills. A good supervisor is organized so that he or she can stay on top of things. People think that a messy desk or office implies that someone is busy. A messy desk or office implies that the person is sloppy, unorganized, and is sooner or later is going to miss an important deadline or misplace an important document.

The ability to delegate tasks to staff: The higher up you advance in local government, the less technical work you will be expected to produce. You need to delegate and only work on the things yourself that you know you will have the time to complete.

The ability to create an "action plan": When assigned a project or initiative, develop an action plan by asking:

- Who needs to know?
- Who needs to participate?
- How much time do I have?

Once these questions have been answered, call a meeting and then run the meeting. The purpose of the meeting will be to:

-define the problem or task at hand

-discuss the problem or task

-ask tough, probing questions

-create assignments

-delegate assignments

-set deadlines

-schedule a follow-up meeting

-create a preliminary agenda for the follow-up meeting so that everybody knows what needs to be done between now and then

Make sure all who are in attendance have contributed in the meeting: an idea, a question, or a suggestion. Make adjustments to the action plan as deemed appropriate or as progress on the initiative or task is made. "Sounds like you're asking me to micromanage." Things don't get done at the city or county if somebody isn't micromanaging.

The ability to solve problems: A good supervisor doesn't procrastinate, won't overanalyze a problem, and is a logical thinker.

The ability to make decisions: An effective city or county supervisor\director makes decisions. While this sounds easy, it is one of the most difficult things the person at the top has to do. Some decisions should be made quickly. Some decisions should only be made after careful thought and deliberation. Some decisions don't have to be made at all. Never make a decision based on emotions. When asked to make a decision, don't let the person(s) force you into making a quick decision if you don't have to. There is an old saying, "Your lack of planning doesn't make this my emergency." Make sure you have all the facts straight before you act. Remember, if the decision is yours then, ultimately, so is the responsibility for it. Once the decision is made, implement it quickly. You will always be second-guessed by others, but don't leave time for you to second-guess yourself. If it was the right decision, time will tell. If it was the wrong decision, you can always make changes. Look out for opportune times to make a decision. For example, a crisis or other situation may occur that gives you the opening you need to make a difficult decision you have been avoiding or putting off.

Some helpful hints in making decisions:

Pros vs. Cons

Worst-case scenario vs. best-case scenario

Do the pros outweigh the cons?

Does the worst-case scenario outweigh the best-case scenario?

Is there an alternative?

Has something like this ever happened before?

How was it handled?

What's the difference between this situation and that one?

Is there somebody you can talk to about this before deciding?

Do you need to make this decision now?

How much time do you have?

When having to make a quick decision, pay attention to your instinct and conscience. You have been put in your position at the city or county because you have an expertise in a particular area. I was taught this by my Corrections director. There were times when she would notify me that she was going to take a certain action at our county jail based on a hunch she had. She explained to me that when it comes to corrections, she has a "sixth sense" about things. She was right. I read somewhere that our mind retains everything that has ever happened to us, every smell, touch, experience. So it's easy to understand and believe that after spending over twenty-five years in the corrections field, she has developed this sixth sense. We all have this sixth sense in our area of expertise. Your instinct is based on your years of experience, so don't be afraid to go for it and make the call.

After a decision is made, there needs to be follow-up.

Some of the most difficult decisions in local government are personnel decisions. Hiring decisions at best are 50/50. It is important that you do your due diligence in checking references and talking to people who may know the person you are considering hiring. I have worked with exceptional employees who don't interview well, and I've had to transfer or terminate employees who knocked my socks off in their interview. A personnel decision is also a good example of a decision that can be changed or corrected. Most local governments have a probationary period. Take advantage of this. If your organization's probationary period is six months, then make it a point to know if this employee is going to work out within three months. Present your new hire a memo her first day on the job outlining specific projects she will be responsible for and other expectations. Then spend the next month or two observing and coaching her. If problems arise, bring them to her attention immediately. Attempt to correct problems early on. Termination decisions are difficult and should be an absolute last option. Make sure you are working with your Human Resources Department and it supports your decision. As soon as you suspect a problem, no matter how minor, you need to contact your Human Resources Department and follow their instructions. Many times over my career, I have seen supervisors who had gotten fed up with an employee and were ready to terminate only to be sent back and told to start at square one with a write-up—or whatever the first step in a long, progressive, disciplinary process was—because instead of addressing the problem head on and immediately, the boss procrastinated or hoped that the problem would correct itself over time. Most problems, especially personnel-related problems—rarely fix themselves over time.

Presenting to the Governing Body and Elected Officials

As a middle manager you will now be expected to make presentations to the governing body. The rules are:

1. Be brief and stick to the point.
2. Let them ask the questions and don't be afraid to respond with a simple "yes" or "no."
3. Be prepared.
4. If you don't know the answer, say you don't know the answer.
5. Don't ever lie to the governing body about anything.
6. Don't try to outthink them and assume where they are going with their line of questioning. Many times they already know the answer but want you to say it for the public to hear it and to later use to justify their decision.

When giving advice to my staff about presenting to the governing body, I use ice cream to get my point across. We all take turns telling each other what our favorite flavor of ice cream is, and when it is my turn I tell them mine is vanilla. Not very exciting and not full of all kinds of flavor or colors, but it is still sweet. I tell them to think of vanilla ice cream whenever they have to make a presentation to the governing body, and they will be all right.

Preparing for the Next Level

If you want to prepare yourself for a future leadership role in local government beyond middle management, you're going to have to

- Learn your department budget.
- Learn the city or county's budget.
- Learn the city or county's budget development process.
- Watch and learn how to develop policies and procedures.
- Learn to implement policies and procedures you do not agree with without letting anybody know you are not in agreement.
- Learn to give your boss all the credit, even though you did all the work.
- Learn to respect and accept politics, the people and the processes that it involves.
- Continue to practice the Ten Commandments for the local government employee.

Even if you're not interested in a higher position, you increase your value to the local government by knowing and doing the things listed above because you can train your boss. He or she and the governing body will eventually reward you for this.

Part IV: The Local Government Manager / Administrator

The following rules and advice is for the first time city or county manager / administrator.

When I contemplated accepting the job as county manager for Santa Fe County, the best piece of advice I got was "Do you know how to count to three? If not, you better learn real quickly." The Board of County Commissioners for Santa Fe County is made up of five commissioners, so three constitutes a majority. As county manager, I need three votes in order get things done.

Today, when I meet other county or city managers for the first time, the first question we ask one another is, "How high do you have to count?" The higher the poor guy or gal has to count, the harder the job is to do.

The Governing Body

The governing body is your boss. Always keep them in the loop, each of them, and this will ensure that you always stay in their loop. By communicating with them regularly, you always stay one step ahead of your opposition, which sometimes includes your own staff and members of the public.

When making personnel related decisions regarding department directors or other key members of staff, such as hiring, promoting, disciplining, or termination, seek the governing body's input. Make sure you always have a majority who agree with your decision. All elected officials will say they don't micromanage but when it comes to leadership positions or key staff positions in the organization, they do. And that's okay as long as you're always one step ahead.

New Initiatives and Programs

Always propose a new initiative or program to your governing body the same way you introduce solid food to a baby. Start with a small spoon so if they don't like what you're feeding them they can spit it out and it won't make a big mess.

The bigger the initiative or program, the more patience and time you will need to get it approved. Start with an e-mail to introduce the idea. Follow up with one-on-one meetings to provide more detail. Gradually increase the information and build towards presenting action items as they get more comfortable with the proposal. Ideally, at some point, one or two of them will take over and sponsor the measure themselves.

Don't ever get too far ahead of your governing body.

Your Management Team

There are two schools of thought regarding the selection and development of a senior management team. One is get rid of everybody and bring in your own people. The other is to retain and work with the directors that have been there because of the institutional knowledge they possess.

If you have been promoted into the position of county or city manager, then you have the advantage of having worked with these individuals and you know which you can work with and which you cannot. You may not have to make this decision yourself; those that don't have confidence in you will start looking to leave the organization once it's been announced that you are now their boss.

If you are new to the city or county you are taking a much bigger risk retaining senior staff members. The governing body may ask, or in some cases require, that you keep certain individuals on your staff. You may want to keep certain individuals and be asked to get rid of these same individuals. Make sure you know both of these things before you accept the position. There's nothing wrong with having a discussion with the governing body about each existing member of the senior staff during your interview process. If they identify individuals that they want you to retain on your staff that is okay but make it clear to them that these individuals are their pick. You are willing to accept that, but if things don't work out you need the freedom to terminate them. A potential pitfall to retaining existing senior staff is that these individuals may feel a sense of empowerment because they know you were forced to keep them. They may be harder to manage. When there are disagreements with direction you are giving, these individuals you were required to keep may appeal directly to the members of the governing body. If the governing body isn't careful they will undermine your authority and hurt your chances for success. You need to ponder this carefully before accepting the job. If you decide to take the job, don't be surprised if the pitfall I mentioned doesn't happen right away. Consider yourself lucky if it does. It will be easier to remind the governing body about the conversation you had before you accepted the job. More than likely there is going to be a "honeymoon" period in the beginning and things will appear as if all is going to be fine. Don't get caught up in this. If you find yourself having to retain certain members of staff then teambuilding will need to be your top priority in your new job. It will be important for you to keep the governing body informed about the progress you are making with the staff they insisted that you keep. Let them know early on if you think things aren't going to work out but let them know what you are planning to do to try and make it work.

As a city or county administrator you are always going to have to be planting seeds with the governing body. After the seed is planted continue to water it so by the time you have to make a major decision the governing body has seen it grow over time to the point that the decision you have to make is obvious.

Regardless, the three most important people to you in your organization will be the finance director, the attorney, and the human resources director. Keep this in mind when deciding whether or not to accept the position of county or city manager/administrator.

Your senior management team should be diverse in race and gender.

Whatever you decide to do or have the authority to do when it comes to putting together your senior management team, you have to have confidence in each individual member and, more importantly, they have to have confidence in you.

FEAR

> **F**uture
> **E**xpectations that
> **A**ren't
> **R**eal

Just because you are the city administrator now doesn't mean you won't experience fear when you have to make a decision. Once you've made up your mind, fear will still be present. Do what you have to do anyway. The existence of fear is not an indication of whether you are right or wrong.

The Employees

Make it a point during your administration to get to know as many employees as possible. Attend your different department's staff meetings whenever possible. Send e-mail updates on a monthly or quarterly basis city- or countywide, letting the staff know about major projects and initiatives that are being undertaken. Try to attend new employee orientations, introduce yourself to new hires, and tell them about yourself and the organization they are joining. Whenever I introduce myself to new hires at new employee orientation, I let them know that as the county manager, I have an open door policy. I clarify that it is an open door, but it is not a back door. I want to hear about their experience at the county so far and any experiences they have had at other agencies that might enhance or improve our service to each other and the public. I don't want to hear about their personnel-related problems. The lower the level they can solve their personnel-related problem, the better off they will be. Inevitably, an employee will get on my calendar and will start to talk to me about problems he is having with his supervisor. I will hear out the employee and then make it really clear that when it comes to personnel actions, nine and a half times out of ten, the supervisor is right and the employee is wrong. If that weren't the case, then that particular individual would not be in his or her supervisory position. As the county manager, I make sure that my supervisors are well trained, honest, and fair with their employees. If I always have to overturn personnel decisions that my supervisors are making, then I'm not doing a good job as county manager. I assure the employee that with almost twenty years of experience and having been in his shoes and his supervisor's, I think I know what I am talking about. He needs to go back and try to resolve the problem by apologizing and to start doing exactly what his supervisor is requesting with a smile on his face.

Employee Recognition

Employee recognition in your organization should be treated as seriously and acted on officially the same way as employee discipline. At Santa Fe County, we have an "Employee Disciplinary Action Form." We warn employees with this form, we give them a written reprimand with this form, we suspend and terminate employees with this form. The form consists of a top white page, a yellow copy for the Human Resources Department, and a pink copy for the employee. At the top of the form, there are several categories or reasons for the disciplinary action (i.e., insubordination, conduct tending to interfere with the efficient operation of the workplace, excessive absences, etc.). At the bottom of the form, there is a signature line for the Employee, the Supervisor, the Department Director, the Human Resources director, and the County Manager. When I became county manager, I made my Human Resources Department create an "Employee Recognition Form." The form consists of a top white page, a yellow copy for the Human Resources Department, and a pink copy for the employee. At the top of the form, there are several categories or reasons for the recognition (i.e., received a positive comment about the employee from a member of the public, completed a project ahead of schedule and within budget, etc.). At the bottom of the form, there is a signature line for the Employee, the Supervisor, the Department Director, the Human Resources director, and the County Manager. You get my point.

Employee Development

Create an employee development program with training programs that target the specific needs of your employees and your organization. Create a series of customer service trainings for specific job areas and fields. Use those staff members to create the training program. For example, at Santa Fe County, we had all of the administrative staff, secretaries, receptionists, and administrative assistants meet regularly and develop their own customer service training course. Create a middle-management team and have them develop training courses for middle managers and first-time supervisors. Besides specific trainings, another advantage of having these groups or teams is the peer support it creates. This helps with morale, which ultimately will have a positive effect on the service you're providing, which ultimately is why local government exists. Ensure that your employees are participating in the trainings by incorporating a "attended training" category on your city or county employee annual performance review form. Add an, "All employees under your supervision have attended at least [no.] of trainings," category to your supervisors' annual performance review form.

You may be able to use members or your community to help you with employee trainings. For example, I once asked my former high school football coach to come and speak to my employees about teamwork.

Partner with your local community college or technical institute to develop training courses and schooling for your employees.

Always be on the lookout for opportunities to make your local government one where today's animal control officer is tomorrow's city or county manager.

PART V: MISCILANEOUS OBSERVATIONS AND THOUGHTS FROM EIGHTEEN YEARS OF LOCAL GOVERNMENT EXPERIENCE

- Local government employees love to gossip, so learn to keep information to yourself.
- The higher you advance in local government, the smaller your circle of trust becomes.
- The less you know about your boss's personal life the better. The less she knows about yours, the better.
- Never underestimate an elected official.
- Never underestimate your boss.
- Don't accept an "at-will" appointed position too soon in your career.
- The higher up you advance in local government, the more you need to understand and respect local politics and the people who participate in them.

- The latest buzz words in local government are *transparency*, *strategic planning*, and *interest-based bargaining*.
  - o *Transparency* depends on the situation and could deter you from making the right decision.
  - o *Strategic-planning* doesn't mean much if it isn't reflected in the organizations annual operating budget.
  - o *Interest-based bargaining* will work only if labor trusts management. The fact that there is a union probably is a good indication that labor doesn't trust management.
- Local government employees think they know politics. They don't.
- If you're going to be successful as the local government administrator you better "know how to count." The higher you have to count, the harder the job.
- The easiest employees to supervise in local government are the line staff. The most difficult employees to supervise in local government are the middle managers. Middle managers think it's their job to say "no."
- The hardest decisions in local government are personnel decisions.
- The definition of a "leader" in its most basic form is someone who serves others. Therefore, all city and county employees are leaders regardless of their position on the organizational chart.

ABOUT THE AUTHOR

At the time of the first printing of this book Roman R. Abeyta was the Santa Fe County Manager, Santa Fe County , New Mexico, USA. Santa Fe County has a population of 140,000. The organization has 900 employees, a governing body that consists of five elected County Commissioners and six independently elected officials (Sheriff, Assessor, Treasurer, Probate Judge, Clerk, Surveyor). Roman began his career in local government at 18 years old working for Santa Fe County as an Animal Control Officer. After working for Animal Control for five months he spent the next ten years in the Planning and Land Use Department working his way up through the department to become the Planning and Land Use Director. After two and a half years as the Planning and Land Use Director he was promoted to Deputy County Manager. In May 2006 Roman was appointed by City of Santa Fe Mayor David Coss to the City's Deputy City Manager position, but then returned shortly thereafter to Santa Fe County to accept an appointment as the Santa Fe County Manager. Over a 15 year period he literally worked his way up from the very bottom of the County organizational structure to the top. He is a real life local government success story. He is married to Geraldine Gurule from Santa Fe, New Mexico and together they have two sons Dillon and Joshua. Roman has two older sons from a previous marriage Roman Aaron Abeyta and Jacob Abeyta and he is the step father to Jimmy Tapia.

14170702R00058

Made in the USA
Lexington, KY
16 March 2012